URBANITY FAIR

An Abbreviated guide to modern manners

URBAN'ITY n. – Etiquette, manners, charm, class, culture, dignity, distinction, grace, politeness, refinement, style.

URBAN'ITY FAIR n. – A fun, fulfilling life-style led with charm, grace & dignity.

Cover Artwork by Kinley Winnaman
Illustrations by Colin Perry

To my "Todo" Jim,
Frankie & Ella, & my
exquisite mother Phyllis

Table of Contents

Preface

Why is having good manners important? Having good manners is important because it is a way of showing respect and appreciation for others, as well as for yourself. I always like to say that respect, begets respect. Etiquette is more about being kind, gracious, and considerate of others, than it is about how you use your knife and fork. It means being a decent human being and following the golden rule. Treat other people as you would wish to be treated. Etiquette is a code of ethics. These ethics help make you a better, more trusted and respected individual. They build friendships, relationships, careers, and open doors. The word "etiquette" means "ticket" in French. Having good manners is your ticket to go anywhere in the world, interact with anyone, and feel confident, accepted and secure in yourself. It gives you a greater sense of self-esteem. Having good etiquette will get you noticed far more than any tattoo, piercing, funky hair color, low-cut blouse, short skirt, low ride pants, or personal posting. Good manners will not only get you the attention of others, but you'll be noticed for all of the right reasons! "Urbanity," means to be "Urbane," or polite and confident. I hope this book will help you to be just that, and so much more.

Urbanity Fair is an abbreviated guide to modern manners. I have chosen to highlight basic etiquette, which is missing in today's society. It is everything you should know about etiquette, but are too afraid to ask. We will explore the many facets of etiquette, with an emphasis on poise, dining etiquette and social skills. For more information on subjects not covered here, I suggest that you explore the Internet and buy or download books from experts such as Emily Post, Letitia Baldrige or Dorothea Johnson.

Be different! Be Urbane!

Personal Carriage & Posture

The first thing that anyone will notice when you walk into a room is how you carry yourself. Studies have proven that people who have good posture are thought to be more powerful. They also appear to be taller and thinner than they actually are. Work on your posture and get rid of bad habits. Don't slouch, shuffle your feet while walking, sit down like a gorilla or sit with your legs apart!

DO NOT SIT WITH YOUR LEGS APART! Mr. & Mrs. Knees are so in love, that they must never be apart. Ladies especially, should never sit without Mr. & Mrs. Knees together!

1. Make it a habit to hold your stomach in at all times. This will keep you from folding over and slouching.

2. Stand up straight with your shoulders relaxed and upright. Pretend that there is an invisible string going from your belly button to the top of your head. Feel as though you are being lifted up by that invisible string, making you feel lighter and taller. Also imagine another string from your belly button through your back, pulling in your tummy.

Picture a guardian angel holding you up like a puppet on a string. I call my angel "Clarence!"

3. When you feel that you are slouching, shrug your shoulders as hard as you can up to your ears, hold for 5-10 seconds, and release. You will see that your shoulders will naturally fall into alignment. This is also a good exercise to do to relax, or to calm you down before you make an entrance.

4. Walk with one foot in front of the other. Do not shuffle your feet, but pick them up and walk heel to toe. Make an effort to glide! Use your knees to stop you from bouncing and swaying. Pretend your knees are like the shocks on a car. Let them absorb all of the bumps so you can walk smoothly.

5. Don't slam yourself down into a chair, or bend from your torso while sitting. Simply lower yourself straight down and get up the same way.

General Guidelines

1. Good hygiene is a must! Your hair, nails, body, and clothing should be clean and neat. Always dress appropriately and never look disheveled or wear unkempt clothing. Good grooming says that you care about yourself as well as others, so make the effort and show that you care.

"A little powder and a little paint, make a woman what she ain't!"

2. Always maintain good posture. Be proud and hold yourself with pride! Always sit up straight and don't slouch. Keep your back straight, your chin level, and your shoulders relaxed. Instead of thinking about squeezing your shoulder blades together, hold in your stomach. This will keep you upright, and reduce the tension in your back, neck and shoulders. Hold your stomach in, as if you had a string being pulled from your belly button through your back. Getting into the habit of maintaining good posture will help to keep your body in alignment, and your muscles firm. Holding your stomach in, and your muscles firm will prevent you from developing a pouch.

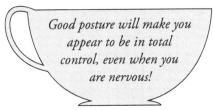
Good posture will make you appear to be in total control, even when you are nervous!

Give it a try Hold in your stomach and then try to slouch. It's impossible!

3. While walking, stand up straight and lead with your chest line and foot. Be sure not to lead with your head, chin or abdomen. Walk purposefully, not pitifully.

4. When you sit down, approach the chair, pivot, and place one foot back, feeling the chair with your calf so you know it is there without looking at it. Slightly lower your torso and sit straight down. Don't bend over and plop down like a sack of potatoes! Once seated, place your hands in your lap and drop your feet to the side. Keep your knees closed, and slightly to the side! Remember about Mr. & Mrs. Knees and how they hate to be apart! You may cross your ankles, but do not cross your legs! Besides, doing so cuts off circulation and causes damage to your veins. When possible enter chairs on the right.

5. Do not sit all the way back in the chair, because it will cause you to slouch. Sitting in the center of the chair will give you better posture. Long ago, they used to put nails on the chair back to prevent children from sitting all the way back in their chair and slouching.

6. When you rise out of the chair, place one foot back to help push yourself up and place your hands on the chair to stabilize yourself. Rise straight up, without leaning forward, especially when rising from being seated at a table. Think about it disaster could occur if you use the table to help you stand up!

7. When getting in and out of a car or limousine, first sit on the seat and then swing both legs in, or out together. Do not separate Mr. and Mrs. Knees and make them sad! Actually doctors say that getting into the habit of swinging your legs as a unit when getting in and out of vehicles will reduce stress and pain in your lower back.

Meetings & Introductions

First impressions are lasting. Regardless of gender, always stand to greet someone. Showing respect is impressive!

Now that you know how to carry yourself, let's work on how to properly introduce yourself, your parents & elders and your friends. There are three important steps to a proper introduction:

1. Use a firm, yet gentle handshake. Never give the limp "cold fish" handshake, nor "grip it and rip it" by grasping their hand with all of your might. Shake hands with a woman only if she extends her hand first. Make a slight move forward, but don't invade someone's personal space. Proper spacing is approximately 18 inches apart. Refrain from using both hands. Be mindful of the duration of the handshake and try not to hold a person's hand too long. Pump hands twice, exchange names and release. Rapid pumping makes you appear nervous.

"The Weirdo Creepy" You may encounter those you may not want too close to you. In this case, instead of slightly moving forward, take a step back. This move will place your leg in front of you as a barrier and will help you to release the grip quicker. Then, take another step back and place your hands to your side. This is a non-verbal way of communicating that they are invading your space and need to step back.

2. Maintain constant eye contact. The person you are meeting deserves your full attention. Rather than looking down, or away from the person, look directly into their eyes. Please avoid looking over their shoulder to see if someone else of more importance has entered the room. The person you are meeting deserves your full attention.

3. State your name and repeat theirs. Think about it, how many times are you introduced to someone and they simply say, "Hi, nice to meet you." You are left without knowing their name, and you either don't state yours at all, "I'm fine thanks, nice to meet you too," or you awkwardly ask them to tell you their name. Therefore, you've totally lost the point of the introduction in the first place! Keep in mind – often times it is not what you know, but whom you know! Repeating the name of the person you just met will help you to remember it. You may still forget their name, but don't be afraid to simply ask for their name again. In most cases you'll find that they have also forgotten yours, and after all, to err is human.

General Guidelines

1. When introducing people, remember to address ladies first, or the person with the most authority. Turn to that person first and then introduce them. In most business or social situations, you can be safe by remembering to introduce the woman, or the person with greater authority, to your guest, or the person with lesser authority. For example, when introducing your girlfriend or boyfriend to your parents, you must first acknowledge your mother, and then your father: "Mom and dad, I would like you to meet my friend Mary Brown; Mary, these are my parents Jane and John Winn." Use this example for most of your introductions, and it may be helpful to get into the habit of saying, "_____I would like to introduce to you_____," or "_____this is___." You can fill in the blanks with the obvious names and titles. Always state the person's title, and use first and last names. It is also a good idea to state their relation to you, i.e. – friend, cousin, etc.

2. Parents especially, should not introduce adults to children by their first name. Do not say, "Hi Julie Ann, this is my son Frank. Frank, this is Julie Ann." It is implying that your child is a part of your adult peer group, which is absurd. When parents do this to me I shake hands with the child and say, "Hello it is nice to meet you Frank. My name is Mrs. Ulcickas, but you may call me Mrs. U." When it comes time for an adult to tell a child to call them by their first name, this should be based on a relationship founded upon mutual respect. It is a right of passage that should not be taken away.

3. Say, "Hello," "It's a pleasure to meet you," or "It's nice to meet you," and state their name.

4. Ask how to pronounce their name. My last name is very difficult and can be badly butchered. When people ask me the proper pronunciation, I feel as though they care enough to know. Doing so is a sign of respect.

5. Introduce yourself whenever the situation arises, especially when the name of the person has escaped your companion. Always introduce the person you are with, to a group with which they are not familiar.

6. Always stand when being introduced, if possible.

7. Do not tilt your head to the side or flip your hair. This is a non-verbal form of flirtation. When shaking hands, be careful not to place your index finger down their wrist, as this is also a form of flirtation.

8. Keep your body about 18 inches from the other person. Be mindful of invading another person's space.

9. Name tags are worn on the right, just below the shoulder.

10. When mingling, hold your beverage in your left hand in order to keep your right free to shake hands.

11. Purses are always worn on the left, for the same reason.

Conversation

The best addiction is diction.

Learn to speak softly, and pace your speech so you can be clearly understood. Learn proper grammar and practice it often. This of course, is true for speech as well as writing. Nothing is more immediately noticeable than poor grammar, so please study everything you can find on the Internet about the subject. While speaking, watch out for "um," "gonna," "shoulda," "woulda," etc. Enunciate your words and get used to saying "yes" instead of "yeah."

When asked how you are doing, it is improper to respond with, "I'm good." Rather say, "I'm well."

A good conversationalist is someone who knows how to listen before they speak. What you say says a lot about the type of person you are and naturally, you want the picture to be as nice as possible. Keep things happy and positive. Having a good personality means having a good attitude. Always try to be pleasant and kind to others, and treat them as you would want to be treated.

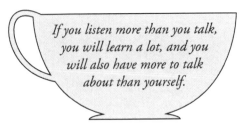

If you listen more than you talk, you will learn a lot, and you will also have more to talk about than yourself.

Stay away from gossip and be the one who makes the best of every situation. Remember the golden rule: "Do unto others as you would have them do unto you."

People are often afraid, or uncomfortable to enter into conversation, especially in social settings. The best thing to do before you start any conversation is to listen. Before you start in on a conversation, listen to what they are talking about, and gather ideas about what you would like to say. It is often a good idea to start by asking a question, as it is no secret that people like to talk about themselves, or about something they know. Asking others questions about themselves can often lead into interesting topics of conversation, and you may also find that you have quite a bit in common. However, do not bombard the person with too many questions, and please avoid talking about yourself all of the time. The key to everything in life is balance, and conversation is certainly no exception. Before you know it, people will think that you are a great conversationalist, when you have only practiced good listening skills.

Conversations should not revolve around social media. Think about what is truly important to you in life. Is it what is happening in cyberspace, or is it your interpersonal relationships with the people in your present company? Remember, unlike humans, the internet will always be there. Use your time wisely.

- Do not rudely interrupt a conversation. Wait until there is a lull in the conversation to chime in.
- Do not one up others during conversation. Always saying, "So did I", "Me too", etc. is boring, not to mention conceited. Allow people to tell <u>their</u> story.
- Never repeat damaging gossip or say mean things about other people. Others will learn not to trust you and you will end up with no true friends.
- Refrain from speaking about politics, race, or religion.
- Refrain from using profanity.
- Never speak about money or discuss prices, outside of business coversations.
- Never ask personal questions regarding age, weight, etc., nor assume that someone is pregnant.
- Bow out gracefully. Say something nice and excuse yourself before leaving a conversation.

Common Courtesies

Unlock the door to true happiness
with kindness, respect & appreciation.

Always demonstrate respect and kindness for others. Try never to be rude, condescending, and never gossip. Common courtesies and general rules of conduct are all common sense. There is a logical reason for every rule, yet they all stem from the Golden Rule: Do unto others, as you would have them do unto you. As human beings, it is our duty to be the best we can be to ourselves, as well as others. Rise above! Be a little kinder, and a little better. Practice, and live by these common courtesies and general rules of conduct. You will soon realize the respect you will receive, and more importantly, you will respect yourself.

- Say "thank you" and "please" every chance you get, to anyone and everyone. Appreciation goes a long way, in every way.
- Learn to smile and say "hello!"
- Always hold a door open for the next person to pass through and remember "please," "thank you," "you're welcome" and "pardon me."
- A gentleman should always open a door for a lady, and allow her to walk in first. Always assist a lady with her chair, and stand when she leaves the room or returns. A lady allows a gentleman to do this for her. Please try to keep chivalry alive and well!
- Always acknowledge and thank anyone who stands for you at a table, stands for you to get by them, or opens a door for you.
- While walking on a sidewalk, allow people enough room to pass easily, and lend the way to the elderly and women. If you accidentally bump into someone – please apologize!
- Practice patience! Take a deep breath and try to smile, rather than lose your cool.
- Endeavor to be on time or early for all appointments.
- For parties you may show up a few minutes late, but do not

exceed 15-20 minutes. Contact your host if you know you are going to be more than a few minutes late.

- Never cough, sneeze or yawn without turning your head away from others, into a cupped hand or tissue.
- Children should not call adults by their first name unless otherwise told to do so. It shows a tremendous lack of respect.
- Never call attention to yourself in public. Try not to point, call out a name, or summon a server from across a restaurant.
- Never be rude or unkind to those in service positions. Always say "please" and "thank you."
- Do not chew gum in public! If you are chewing it in your car and need to get rid of it before you're seen, discreetly put it into a trashcan instead of on the ground. Never stick it under a chair or table!
- Never litter!
- Leave everything cleaner than when you found it, including restrooms, dressing rooms, and other public places.
- In restrooms, if others are available do not use the handycapped stall.
- While trying on clothes in dressing rooms, do not throw garnments on the floor and make every effort to re-hang the clothing you tried on. Always leave a dressing room as though you were never there.
- Do not brush your hair in public, especially near a table or where food is served.
- Do not wear hats, such as ball caps in restaurants or places of worship.
- Remember: If you think that something may be rude or offensive – do not do it, because it probably will be! Always try to use common courtesies when dealing with others!
- Always make an attempt to use proper manners. If you ever have a question regarding what to do in a particular situation, email me and I will be glad to help you!
- Remember to try and be respectful, gracious, kind and charming!

The Girlfriend's Code of Ethics
"GCE"

Women need to stick together and help each other out whenever possible. Regardless of your background, race or religion, we have the same biological challenges, and we feel the same emotions. Each of us deserves compassion and understanding, often something one can only get from another girlfriend. Be there for each other. Be a comfort, not a critic. Show your support when a girlfriend needs some extra self-esteem. Build her up, and be the girlfriend you would want someone to be to you. The Girlfriend's Code of Ethics has no room for gossip, jealousy, or under-handed disloyalty. Remember, a good friend can be trusted to keep a secret. Silence is a golden "GCE" egg.

- A girlfriend is trustworthy and she has your back.
- She is protective of you, your family and of your reputation.
- She is a good listener.
- She is never jealous, but truly happy for another's successes.
- She would never covet another's mate.
- She is helpful and there when you need her.
- She never gossips or is unkind.
- She is a woman of her word.
- She does not embarrass you in front of others or online.
- She truly cares about your health and happiness.

Cyberquette

While I realize the relevence of computers in today's society, they cannot run themselves. Humans will not cease to exist because of technology, so it is of vital importance that we honor and practice the art of communication. We are social beings by nature, so we must nurture this part of ourselves in order to create and enhance relationships. After all, it is these relationships that bring us happiness. If we allow technology to take away this part of our true selves, we might as well revert back to being apes.

Just say no to the phone – or you might as well be alone!

In a world where everyone seems to post every move they make, cyber safety is critical. Everything you put online can come back to haunt you – everything. Nothing in cyberspace can be completely eradicated, and can be used against you. When you apply for a school, interview for a job, apply for membership of a club, etc., the first thing people will do is Google you. Even innocent postings can be misconstrued. Being the target of cyber-bullying, can be devastating.

- As hard as it may seem, refrain from using your cell phone while in the company of others. The people in your present company deserve your attention, not those in cyberspace!

- Phones must always be silenced or turned off when dining with others.
- Phones are never placed on a table during a meal. They are silenced, and kept in your purse or pocket. They may be brought out to show or take photos, but keep them off of the table.
- Texting under the table is rude. You think you're being sly, but everyone knows what you are doing!
- Keep posting to a minimum. Not everyone needs to know your every move, and certainly not every meal you've eaten. Besides being TMI (Too Much Information), it can be dangerous. Anyone can see where you are and what you're doing at any given moment, which lends itself to the "weirdo creepies" out there who want to do you harm. Many times houses are burglarized because the family has posted that they are out of town.
- Place a sticker or a band aid over your computer's camera when not in use, especially if it's in your bedroom. International hackers can hack into your computer's camera and watch you from anywhere in the world.
- Provocative pictures and foul language are absolutely prohibited! If you do, plan on it coming back to haunt you. Be aware that if someone is trying to find out information about you, they will not just look at you content, but also that of your friends.
- Never post uncomplimentary photos or content of others. Making someone look bad online is evil and a mark of insecurity.
- If you wouldn't say it to their face, don't say it online!
- Emails should be brief and to the point, not rambling.
- Read through all of your emails before responding, because there may be updates to the original email sent at a later time.
- Always respond to an email. Even a quick, "Thank you" should be sent so the person knows you have read it and are responsive.
- Never put anything on the Internet that you would not want your parents or children to see!

Out On The Town

- Call or ask for a date in person. Actually SPEAK to them, rather than text or email.
- Do not wait until the last minute to call and ask for a date. If the person is special enough to take out, they deserve a call at least a day or two ahead of time, if not more.
- Establish the terms of the date, including where, when, method of transportation, etc. Make sure your date knows the expected attire. If you are going to your private club, make sure you go over club rules such as never using your cell phone, not wearing jeans, no tipping and so forth.
- Good hygiene is a must! Make sure your hair, nails, body, teeth and clothing are neat and clean. Good grooming says that you care about yourself as well as others. Bad breath is a deal breaker!
- For the younger set, when you pick up a girl at her home, ALWAYS shake hands and introduce yourself to her parents and give them the exact time you will return. Mind the curfew and always be respectful of the parent's rules. Don't speak badly about your parents and their "stupid rules." They love you and are only looking out for your best interest. They not only want to keep you safe, they are also protecting your reputation.
- Chivalry is not dead! A gentleman always opens doors for a lady, including car doors.
- Men usually escort a lady on their left side. Originally this was because men needed to have their right hand free to be able draw their swords which were most commonly worn on their left side. To escort a lady to the dance floor, a gentleman offers his right arm. He is offering his fighting arm in service to his lady. However, modern etiquette dictates that this is no longer nessassary.

- Men should always walk on the outside, or the street side, of a lady.
- Men should walk in front of a lady while going down stairs. This way, he can break her fall if she should stumble. He may also escort her on his arm up and down stairs.
- Standing for a lady when she leaves or returns to the table is now considered passé, but it is still very much appreciated. Always stand when your guest is first approaching the table for the first time.
- The person that extended the invitation and made the arrangements should pay, unless otherwise arranged. Pick something you can afford.
- Turn off or silence your cell phone. Your full attention should be given to your date. If you simply must have it on, keep usage to a minimum. After all, why bother going out with someone if you spend the entire time in cyberspace.

Refrain from using your phone during a date. Use the time to really get to know each other. There is no point of going on a date if you sit and stare at your phone the entire time!

- Do not talk about past relationships.
- Be mindful of prices and refrain from ordering the most expensive items on the menu.
- If you would like to order wine, regardless of price, you should pay for the bottle. This is especially true when dining in groups. Ordering extremely expensive wines and then expecting everyone to split the bill evenly is rude. Everyone should agree upon the wine and the price before ordering if you are splitting the bill.
- If someone is not drinking alcohol and you are splitting the check, give them the option to not charge them for drinks.

Although it is a bit more difficult to figure out the check, it is a very nice gesture that is greatly appreciated.

- Never pressure any party to do something they don't want to do. Never put your date in a dangerous or compromising position. Never do anything illegal, unethical or simply stupid.
- Refrain from PDA's – Public Displays of Affection.
- The parting should be in accordance with the success of the date. If it went well, then a hug or a small kiss is fine. Do not get too affectionate after the first date. Take things slowly and never make someone feel uncomfortable.
- Always say thank you and be appreciative of the time and effort that person put into making a nice outing for you. Even if you had a less-than-perfect experience, say thank you and be gracious.
- Follow up a good date with a phone call, text or email. Let them know you had a good time and hope to see them again.
- Be a person of your word and call when you say you are going to call. If you have no intention of pursuing the relationship, do not make promises you do not intend to keep. Playing games is immature and shows a lack of integrity.

General Guidelines for movies, live performances and restaurants

1. At the movies:
- The man should open the door and let the lady go in first, handing the tickets to the usher behind her.
- When finding seats, the man should lead the lady, holding her hand if it's dark. The lady should go to her seat first, and the man should follow. If you are on a double date, one man should go in first, followed by the two ladies, so that the men flank the ladies on each side.
- Be courteous of those around you and be quiet. Please remember to turn off your cell phones.

- Refrain from putting your feet up on the chair in front of you or touching it in anyway.

2. At theaters or concerts:
- Be punctual! In many theaters you will not be permitted to enter after the performance has started and will have to wait until after the first act.

- When people are passing by you to get to their seat, swivel your knees to the side to allow people *Always face the stage and not the people seated while passing to your seat. Side-step and acknowledge the person you are passing with a nod, a pardon me, excuse me, or thank you.* to pass by, but if it's tight, always be the first to stand. You should also always stand when you see someone who may have difficulty passing due to a physical disability or if they are larger than most. It saves them the embarrassment of having to try and squeeze through.
- Do not clap between movements, but rather wait until the end.
- Do not leave your seat until the act is over and the lights come up. Return to your seat immediately when the warning bell signals the end of intermission.
- Do not eat or drink during a play or concert, and be aware of the performers and do not cause unnecessary disturbances.
- Do not bring babies or children too young to sit still and be quiet. If childeren are present, every effort should be made to ensure they are not disruptive.
- Try your best not to fall asleep! Snoring during a performance is simply out of the question!

3. At restaurants:

- Wait for the headwaiter or hostess to come and show you a table. The lady or ladies then follow the headwaiter, and the men follow them. At many fine restaurants, the waiter or hostess who seats you will place your napkin on your lap for you. This is not because you have forgotten; it is simply a gesture of respect towards you. If you are wearing a dark color, politely ask for a black napkin if available, so the white napkin won't cover you in lint.
- Whenever possible, the lady may tell her escort what she would like, so he can give both orders to the waiter. This is a very nice gesture!

4. Tipping:

- The average amount for tipping is 18%, or 20% for excellent service. When dining in a group of six or more, the waiter will automatically add an 18% gratuity to the bill, so be aware of this, and do not tip twice. You may tip 10% on expensive bottles of wine or champagne. The easiest way to figure the tip is to just double the tax.
- Tips should be given to drivers, restaurant staff, valets, porters and anyone you believe deserves something extra for good service. You should also tip your hairdresser, if they own the salon or not. In the past, owners of salons were not tipped for their services, but that is no longer the case.
- At least $10 per day should be given to household staff if you are a guest at a private home, and it is always nice to leave a token of your appreciation for housekeeping staff in hotels and the like.
- Tip those you see regularly more generously during the holiday season and keep in mind your postal and newspaper delivery, sanitation workers, elevator operators, etc.

General Travel Etiquette

Believe it or not, how you behave while travelling is a direct reflection upon not only yourself and your family, but of your hometown, city, state and country. When you are travelling abroad, in many ways you are acting as a representative of the US. Please do not be the "crude American", and make the rest of us look bad! Honor the sacrifices of our brave men and women in our Armed Forces and uphold the American pride that we should all share. Here are a few things to keep in mind while travelling:

- Before you travel, familiarize yourself with the customs and protocol of where you will be visiting. Know exchange rates and their tipping policies. For instance, tipping in China is considered an insult and only tour guides should be tipped.
- Be mindful of your attire and pack according to the climate, impending weather, occasion, and local customs. Many countries have strict dress codes and you will be seen as a foreign pig if you do not adhere to them. In Italy for instance, it is unacceptable to wear shorts and one should never bare their shoulders, midriff or knees in places of worship.
- When boarding be careful not to hit people with your bags.
- Do not relocate other people's belongings.
- Do not kick the seat in front of you, nor use it to pull yourself up.
- Do not go barefoot on an airplane, especially in the restroom.
- Refrain from personal grooming. Do not brush your hair, pick, cut or paint your nails.
- Do not wear sweats or pajamas on airplanes. There are many ways to be comfortable, yet stylish at the same time.
- Always treat flight attendants and other employees with kindness and respect.
- Speak quietly and make an effort not to disturb others. No one likes to be seated next to a chatterbox!

- Only recline your seat if absolutely necessary. Again, think of the Golden Rule.
- Keep your area clean and neat, and leave it cleaner than you found it. This rule also applies to the restrooms.
- When flying with children, make every effort to keep them from being disruptive. Make sure you have a lot for them to do and plenty to eat and drink. Headphones for children are essential, so others won't be bothered by the sounds of their electronics.
- Often you may see active military flying to or returning from duty. Respect their privacy, but graciously thank them for their service. It is important to note that it is improper for civillians to salute.
- Never yell "Hi" to your friend Jack at the airport! All jokes will be taken seriously and you will end up causing a delay for everyone, not just yourself.

Rules for being a good houseguest:

- Bring a gift for your host. Something from where you live is always nice.
- Be clean and neat. Always make your bed and keep your things tidy.
- Be helpful and offer to pay for at least one meal. Offer to do the dishes or help clean. This is an insult to hostesses in many countries, so make sure to ask before you begin.
- Adhere to their rules regarding hours, animals, etc. Never feed their animals anything unless your host gives you permission!
- Do not show up with anything or anyone your host is not expecting. Bringing your dog or another guest without fully discussing it beforehand is rude!
- Never overstay your welcome! Arrive and leave at the scheduled time, unless it cannot be avoided.

Tips for Taking Photos

Taking pictures and selfies is part of your daily routine, but here is how to do what I call, "The Photopop." The "Photopop" is one fluid motion that will give you an instant make-over and make you look your best. While this may seem overwhelming at first, practice makes perfect!

How to do the "Photopop"

In one instant you simultaneously:

For women:
1. Slightly stick out your chin.
2. Pull in your stomach.
3. Pull back and down your shoulders.
4. Shift your weight to one foot or side if seated.
5. Be aware of your hands and try not to fold or cross them in front of you. Fingers on hips should be together, not splayed.
6. Slightly bend one knee into the other.
7. Place the heel of one foot into the arch of the other.
8. Pop up your heel.
9. Inhale.
10. ¾ Smile with your tongue to the back or your teeth.
11. Look slightly to the side or above the lens.

For men:
1. Slightly stick out your chin.
2. Pull in your stomach.
3. Pull back and down your shoulders.
4. Shift your weight to one foot or side if seated.
5. Be aware of your hands and try not to fold or cross them in front of you.
6. Inhale.
7. ¾ Smile with your tongue to the back or your teeth.
8. Look slightly to the side or above the lens.

Other Tips and Guidelines

1. Practice smiling and find your best angles in the mirror. Take selfies, or have someone photograph you until you have your go-to pose down tight. Remembering to place your tongue to the back of your teeth will give you a perfect smile every time.

2. Standing and looking straight into the lens will add that 10 pounds everyone talks about. Always slightly angle your face and shift your body to the side by distributing your weight to one side.

3. The placement of your hands is very important. They should never be clasped in front of you, nor your arms crossed, unless you're going for an attitude shot. Hands should be down to your side, held slightly away from your body with your elbows bent, so they don't look like part of your waistline. I normally like to put one hand on my waist, but make sure fingers are closed and not splayed. This look cinches in your waist and makes you look thinner.

4. Put one foot in front of the other. This will give you a leaner appearance. I often slightly bend my knee, placing the heel of one foot into the arch of the other.

5. Remain calm and act natural. You want photographs to exude confidence.

6. Lean slightly toward the camera, head first.

7. Be mindful of your wardrobe and your appearance. If you know you will be taking photographs, make sure you have clean hair, skin & nails, that your clothing is neat and clean, and that it fits your figure. Unless you have perfect abs, do not show your mid-drift! Muffin tops are totally unattractive and you'll be embarrassed if the picture becomes public!

8. Solid colors are best. Avoid stripes and patterns, especially for television.

9. When photographing others, do not take the picture with a light source behind your subjects. This will create shadows that may ruin your photos. Also, position your camera above your subjects, angled downward, rather than upward. This will make them appear taller and thinner.

10. "Photo bombing," or jumping into someone else's photo op may be funny to you, but can be really annoying to others. Be mindful of the picture they are taking before you leap in. I have seen many cases where families try to get their kids to cooperate for a photo, only to be ruined by someone leaping in. The moment was lost, and they couldn't get the kids back in order for another photo.

11. When gentlemen pose with a lovely lady for a photo, try to avoid the "Hover Hand," where your hand is hovering slightly above her shoulder or waist. This will make you appear to be nervous, awkward and possibly terrified.

12. Do not assume that someone wants you in a photo. Stand by until you're asked to join. Often people want photos of a specific group.

13. Make sure to make everyone feel important and included. Once you've finished your photo shoot, invite others to join in and make a show of making them feel accepted and important.

14. Obscene gestures, nudity, and other sexy shots are simply never done. Remember that anything you put in cyberspace, stays in cyberspace and can come back to haunt you years later. Never photograph anything you wouldn't want your parents or children to see.

15. Put down glasses and cups before the photo is taken. If it is unavoidable, make sure you are holding stemware by the stem, especially if it is white wine or champagne.

16. When taking selfies, be fully aware of your surroundings. Make sure not to be disruptive or put yourself in a perelous position.

17. A smile is better than a "Duckface."

Correspondence –
The Beautiful Written Word!

Cursive writing is like playing a musical instrument. It connects letters like notes in a song and improves the ability of the brain to focus on details.

- Elaine Weinberg

The written word is perhaps the best form of communication. There is truly nothing more powerful, and nothing reveals your character more plainly than writing. That is why it is of vital importance that your correspondence be done correctly, and that you choose and use your words wisely. Never write anything you should not or do not mean to say, especially on the Internet! The following tips will help you to handle your personal correspondence graciously and properly, creating a positive reflection of your character through your own words.

Written communication has been deemed irrelevant in modern society. In fact, cursive and proper grammar are hardly taught in our schools. Please make every effort to keep the hand written word alive. Hand written notes in cursive are another way of getting you noticed for the right reasons. If you don't know cursive handwriting, there are a multitude of online lessons and resources available. Write On!

Other Tips and Guidelines

1. Use proper grammar! Watch out for the obvious mistakes such as; to and two, you're, your, their, there, they're, etc.

2. Be yourself, and do not try to use words that you would not normally use. Be honest and write from your heart.

3. Make it personal and include details. "Everything was fantastic, from the company to your chicken parmesan!," "I enjoyed hearing about your trip to Japan," etc.

4. Addressing an Envelope:

Always use the first and last name of the recipient. For instance, you would address the envelope Mr. Colin Perry, not just Mr. Perry. Mr. Perry is what you would use on the inside of your note. If you are sending a letter to a person at their place of work, state the company on the first line, and then on the second, write Attn: and the recipients name. This means to bring it to their attention. You may also put the recipient's name on the first line and then "C/O" in front of the company name on the second line. This means "Care Of," or by way of.

- Make sure that you address the envelopes properly. The following is just about all you will need to know:
- Ms. should be used to address a woman, unless she has taken her husband's surname. Using Mrs. with a woman's first name implies that she is divorced. Mrs. is only used with a husband's name.
- A young girl may be called Miss, but single women should be called Ms.
- Boys up to the age of 9 are called Master. Then, between the ages of 10-18, they are called by their first name, or may be called Mr. in more formal situations. After 18, all men are referred to as Mr.
- Married women should be addressed using their husband's surname, unless they have opted to keep their own, or if they possess a title.
- When addressing a married couple, where she has kept her maiden name, the man's name should be written on the first line, followed by the woman's. However, the person with the highest title, professional or educational degree is always placed first.

Return Address

Sally Student
302 Red, White and Blue Ave.
Wilmington, NC 28409

Stamp

Sam Student
405 Liberty Lane
Wilmington, NC 28409

Address

FYI - It is important to note that you only use "and" when the couple is married, and one spouse did not take the other's surname. For instance:

**Ms. Constance Oldham
and Mr. James Van Kleefe
Or
The Honorable James Van Kleefe
and Ms. Constance Oldham**

- For doctors:
  1. If both are doctors:
     **The Doctors Richardson or
     Doctors Angela and Theodore Richardson**

  2. If only the husband is a doctor:
     Dr. and Mrs. Theodore Richardson

3. If only the wife is a doctor, use her professional name if it is different from her married name, but if not, address it to Mr. & Mrs.:

Dr. Angela Clover and Mr. Theodore Richardson
Mr. & Mrs. Theodore Richardson

- For couples living together, write their names in alphabetical order, one above the other, aligned on the left. Do not use "and" because it implies that they are married. It is always proper to put the woman's name first, however, feminist etiquette dictates that the names are alphabetical.

Ms. Melanie Marvelous
Mr. Peter Perfect
Or
Mr. Mike Magnificent
Ms. Sarah Super

- Gay couples are addressed in alphabetical order, unless they are married. There is no plural form of Mr. or Mrs. in the English language. The closest is the French plural for Mr.: Messrs., for Mrs.: Mesdames.
    1. If the couple is unwed:
        Mr. James Connor
        Mr. Ryan Reynolds

    2. If they are married, but kept their surnames:
        Ms. Kelly Clayton
        And Ms. Laura Sharpton

    3. If they are married and took the surname:
        The Messrs. Reynolds
        Or
        The Mesdames Newhart

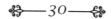

5. E-mails and social media:

The most important thing to know about e-mail is that once it has been sent, you can never take back what you wrote. It can be forwarded over and over, copied, saved and so on. Therefore, it is very important that you never write anything nasty or unkind. Never give out personal information on the Internet. It is simply not safe. E-mails should be short and to the point, because very few people take the time to read long e-mails. The more e-mails, tweets, texts, etc. you send to someone, the less likely they'll be valued.

A little goes a long way.

6. Thank you notes:

Thank you notes are some of your most important letters, and should never be forgotten to be sent. They should be brief and should be sent within a week or two after the occurrence for which you are thankful. I think that you should get into the habit of writing thank you notes whenever someone does something nice for you, because it is the perfect way to show someone that you appreciate their kindness and that you care about them as well. Just be careful not to overdo it, and always be sincere. Consider these following suggestions:

- Thank you notes should be sent within two weeks of receiving a gift, attending a party, going to someone's home for a meal, being a guest on vacation, etc.

Some people equate the length of time it takes to receive a thank you note with the degree of appreciation.

- If a gift was sent to you, such as flowers, you must immediately contact the sender via phone, text, email or social media to let them know you received the gift and that you are grateful. Think about your own concern about the safe arrival of a gift you have sent. It is reassuring to know it arrived. Always follow up with a hand written note, not an email.

- Fill out envelopes beforehand, to remind you to write the note as soon as possible.
- Notes written on behalf of more than one person should only be signed by the writer. It is unnecessary to include multiple names.
- Thank you notes should be written for every gift you receive.
- You may e-mail a thank you note for a meeting, but not for a gift. You may send an e-mail to let someone know you received their gift, but follow it up with a hand-written thank you note.
- Fill in the blank thank you notes are not acceptable, unless you have only just learned how to write. Therefore, if you are over the age of 5, it would not be prudent.
- You must write a thank you note, even if you did not like the gift. Remember that all gifts take time to find and money to buy. Be thankful that someone cares enough about you to do something special for you.
- Keep it short and sweet. State what you are thankful for, how you will use it and what that person or your time together meant to you.
- Make sure to keep a log of your notes. Include the date, to whom the note is written and the act of kindness. This will help you keep track of your correspondence so you do not forget or duplicate.
- Salutations should reflect your relationship to the recipient. "Love," "Love always," "Fondly," etc. are reserved for family members and people closest to you. For all others, use "Sincerely," "Warmly," "Kindly," etc.

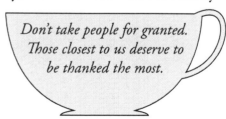

Don't take people for granted. Those closest to us deserve to be thanked the most.

- The body of a thank you note should contain:
    1. The item for which you are thankful. Refrain from using generalized comments like, "thank you for the gift." Otherwise, the recipient may wonder if you really are aware of what they gave you.
    2. A description of how you will use the gift or what it means to you.
    3. Include something personal about the person. Let them know you enjoyed their conversation, that they are an excellent cook, a great friend, a wonderful person, mother, father, grandparent, etc. Make them feel good about themselves and about your relationship.
    4. A closing statement such as, "I look forward to seeing you again."
    5. Briefly thank them again for their kindness.

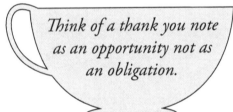

Think of a thank you note as an opportunity not as an obligation.

Sample Thank You Notes

Date

Dear Grandma,

Thank you so much for the money you gave me for my birthday. I promise to use it wisely, or save it, just like you told me to do. Maybe I can save enough for a new bike!

Thank you for always thinking of me on my birthday and for being so generous to me. **You're** the best Grandmother in the whole world! I can't wait to see you again!

Love always,
Your Signature

Please note the correct grammatical use of *you're vs. your.* You're is a contraction and stands for you are. Your is a possessive adjective. Also watch out for *their, there, they're* and the like.

Date

Dear Mr. Perry,

Thank you so much for your time and expertise. I have really enjoyed working with you and because of you, my book may have a chance at success.

I think you are a wonderful person and hope that we will have a continued friendship. Again, thank you for all of your help.

Sincerely,
Julie Ann

Note that you begin a note with either their first name only, or their title and only last name. You would not say, "Dear Mr. Colin Perry," but rather, "Dear Mr. Perry" or "Dear Colin."

Invitations

Invitations may be sent via any method you choose. However, formal invitations are always sent via the good old US Postal Service. If you are having a child's party, you can bring invitations to school ONLY if you are going to invite your whole class. Otherwise, the invitations should be individually sent in the mail or e-mailed. Do not talk about the party in front of others unless you are positive that everyone present is invited. Making someone feel left out is rude!

RSVPs:

- When you receive an invitation, YOU MUST RSVP by the date requested to do so. RSVP means "**R**espondez **S**'il **V**ous **P**lait." which is French for "Please reply." Never show up to a party without responding to the invitation! Never say that you will attend and then not show up! Only guests named on the envelope are invited. Do not assume that you can bring siblings, friends, or a whole entourage. Always communicate directly with your host if you have any questions. Go straight to the source, rather than conjecture with a friend. Chances are, that friend may not have been invited.

- If an invitation says, "Regrets Only," I still like to contact the host. You can send a quick email or other message saying that you received their kind invitation, that you will attend, and ask if there is anything you can do to help. Personally, I don't recommend "Regrets Only," because most people these days do not RSVP at all – tisk tisk!

If you have any questions, communicate with your host. I believe that the only stupid question is the one you didn't ask.

> ### *"The Better Deal"*
> Never accept an invitation and then decline because you received a better offer. Remember that people will most likely be posting pictures that your original host will see and you will hurt their feelings.

General Guidelines

1. Dress according to the tone of the invitation. A formal, engraved invitation does not lend itself to jeans and a t-shirt. If you are unclear about the dress code, especially if the event is to be held at a private club, ask your host. You don't want to be turned away at the door or given a poorly fitting coat and tie!

2. Always bring a hostess gift to a party. It could be a framed picture you took, a card, a flower, plant, etc. It is always nice to let your host know that you are thankful for their hospitality and for being included. My husband and I always bring fresh eggs to our hosts. We have chickens, so it's a special way to share a part of our home and show our appreciation for inviting us to theirs.

3. If you are the guest of honor, it is absolutely imperative that you bring a special gift to your hosts, and make every effort to thank them for their generosity and kindness. On the day after the event, email, call or text them to tell them what a wonderful time you had and thank them for everything they did for you. Then, follow up with a hand written thank you note ASAP. Flowers, framed pictures, or a photo album of the event would also be nice ideas. Make them feel appreciated, and they will feel you were deserving of their efforts.

4. If you would like to initiate a celebration at a restaurant or other venue, but do not wish to be the sole host, make sure that everyone invited knows that they will be responsible to pay for themselves. Not making this clear beforehand will cause great discomfort and confusion.

Dining Etiquette

While at a dining table, people sitting with you or at tables near you, may likely notice your dining etiquette. Therefore, if you have good table manners, their image of you will be positive, and you will save yourself from embarrassing situations. Remember that practice makes perfect, so you should use proper manners even if you are dining alone, so that it will come to you naturally during social events.

Entering the Table

1. Wait until your host or hostess is seated before you sit down. Men should help seat their hostess and all other ladies by pulling out their chair. Ladies are always seated first. A place card may specify where you should sit. If not, ask where they would like you to be seated.

2. Never move your place card! Your host made quite an effort to put together the perfect guest list and table arrangement. Changing it means that you don't trust their judgment.

3. If possible, a man should pull out a chair for a lady on his right. Take care to push in the chair from the mid section, using one leg to assist if needed. Pushing the chair in from the top will topple the lady into the table.

4. When being seated, a lady should hover slightly above the chair, with one foot in front of the other, and pull the chair inward. Keep your body upright and do not bend toward the table.

5. Never hop and scoot your chair!

6. Refrain from putting any personal items on the tabletop. Small purses can be placed on your lap under your napkin, or on the chair behind your back. Other items may be placed on an empty chair, or safely tucked under your feet. Hanging purses on the back of your chair is inviting theft.

7. Do not take out your phone and place it on the table. Remember to silence it and only bring it out if you'd like to take a picture, show someone a picture, or check your calendar if you are making a date with the people in your present company.

The people in your present company deserve your attention, NOT the person in cyberspace!

8. If you know people at other tables in the room, acknowledge them with a polite "hello" or a wave. Do not interrupt their table conversation or dining experience unless you are invited to join them. Even then make it a short and sweet visit.

9. When someone joins the table, stand to greet them and introduce yourself if possible. Never sit to greet someone if you can easily stand. If you cannot, apologize for not standing. This now applies to both men and women.

10. At events, where you may not know everyone at your table, introduce yourself, especially those seated next to you.

11. Make sure to us the restroom before you sit down at the table. Not only is it necessary to wash your hands, it is best not to leave the table during a meal if it can be avoided.

Never put scented candles on a dining table because they will interfere with the aroma of the cuisine.

Fun fact - Centerpieces should be above, or below eye-level. Never make your guests crane their necks around the centerpiece in order to see you. Don't forget that the reason for gathering people together is to converse and enjoy the present company. An imposing centerpiece will do nothing but impede the conversation.

Navigating a Table

There are three ways to navigate the dining table, whether you are the host setting the table, or the guest.

1. Make a "b" with your left hand, and a "d" with your right, (inconspicuously if you're at the dining table). The "b," stands for bread, the "d" for drink. Your bread and butter plate is on the left, your drinks are on the right. From there, you can navigate down to the position of your utensils. Your forks are on the left, knives and spoons on the right.

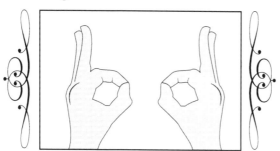

2. A "BMW" is not just a fine automobile. It can also serve as your cue to remember the placement of your **B**read, **M**eal & **W**ater!

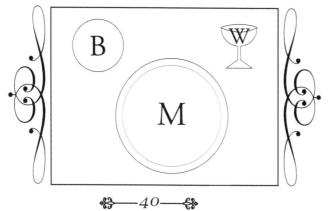

3. 4 letters are in L-E-F-T. Everything with 4 letters goes on the left. F-O-O-D, F-O-R-K. Your bread is FOOD, and therefore goes on the LEFT. During seated dining events with a program, you may be served all courses of a meal at the same time, in order to keep service noise down to a minimum during speeches and performances. Anything FOOD related goes on your LEFT, including salads and desserts.

Normal Place Setting

Mr. Napkin

1. Mr. Napkin is your best friend at the table! He is always used to delicately wipe your mouth and hands, rather than using the back of your hand, your sleeve, shoulder or the tablecloth!

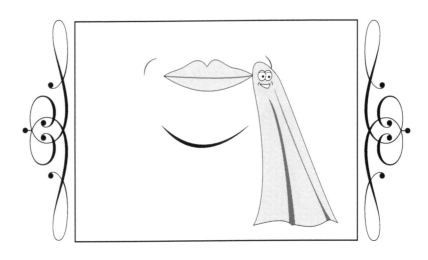

2. Place your napkin across your lap the moment you sit down. You will find Mr. Napkin to the left of your plate, on your plate, or in your beverage glass at the top right of your setting. Never take a napkin further than the right of your glass, because it belongs to the person to your right.

3. Often you may find a "roll up," where your utensils are rolled up inside of a napkin. Unroll the napkin beneath the table and place your utensils in their proper positions.

4. Mr. Napkin is always half folded, either in a rectangle or a triangle. He is never tucked into your collar.

5. A napkin is always taken and unfolded under the table, never above and waived about.

6. During lunch, the napkin may be fully unfolded and laid in your lap, and during dinner, it should be folded in half. I always prefer my napkin half folded across my lap, for both lunch and dinner, however, it is usually completely unfolded during tea.

7. Should you need to excuse yourself from the table during a meal, place your napkin on the chair, not on the table. Always pinch the napkin in the center, and smooth it down. Please do not wad it into a ball. A used napkin never goes on the table while people are still eating, or while food is being served.

8. When you excuse yourself momentarily from the table, say, "Excuse me." Refrain from telling anyone what you are planning on doing in the restroom, if that is where you are headed.

9. When everyone is finished and you are ready to leave, place the napkin on top of the table, to the left of your plate. You may put the napkin back into the napkin ring if so desired, but please

do not wad up your napkin and throw it on top of your plate! During speeches and programs during events, your napkin must remain on your lap, even though you've finished your meal. Your napkin is only placed back on the table, to the left of your plate, when everyone at the table is getting up to leave. If you are getting up to give a speech, it goes on your chair.

Beyonce could be singing **Irreplaceable** *about Mr. Napkin. "To the left - to the left"!*

10. At restaurants and in public places, you may politely ask a server for another napkin if it falls on the floor. In private homes, discreetly pick it up and place it back on your lap.

Before You Dine

1. Once you are seated and your napkin is on your lap, you may begin to sip your beverage and eat your bread. Wait until everyone is seated to begin eating anything else on the table. If you are unsure if more guests will be joining the table, and there is no apparent host at the table, say something to your table mates to indicate that it is all right to begin eating. However, if there is a printed program, check to see if there will be an invocation. If so, you must wait to begin eating until after the blessing.

2. At private parties , begin eating only when your host or hostess is served, and has picked up their fork. If the food is served hot, the host or hostess may tell you to begin eating. Never start eating or drinking anything on the table until you have had an indication to begin. Again, be mindful of blessings or toasts to be made, before you begin to eat.

3. Silverware is served in the order of the courses to be served, starting from the outside working in. The small fork and spoon that you will often find at the top of your plate are for dessert, and should not be touched until dessert is served.

4. Your bread and butter plate is always to the left of your plate. The butter knife may be laid across it or to the right on top of your plate, with the cutting edge facing inward, never out. When passed the butter, only take the amount you will need and swipe it on the right of the plate, with the handle in the hand, finger on the top of your butter knife.

5. Start by tearing the whole roll in half, then again, and then break a bite-size portion off of that. Use your butter knife, or one you have available to swipe the butter on your one bite sized piece. Remember, handle in the hand, finger on the top. Only use one to two swipes and avoid swiping with both sides several times. The rhythm should be tear - swipe - knife down - mouth. You must place your knife down, to the right of the bread plate, with the serrated edge facing inward, before you put the bread into your mouth. You should never have your knife and a piece of bread in your hands at the same time.

6. Never move your bread plate in front of you and always tear your bread over your plate.

> Never butter your entire roll or a piece of bread and eat it whole, or cut your roll in half with your knife, butter the center, and then eat it like a hamburger! Always break off a bite-size portion, butter it if you wish, and put the whole piece into your mouth.

7. Garlic bread, or other breads with spreads or cheeses already on them, can be eaten from the whole, as it is too messy to break it apart. Often times the person seated to your left takes your

bread & butter plate because they are unaware that it is to the left of your plate, not your right. If this happens, do not embarrass them by calling attention to their mistake, but simply place your bread on the upper left of your plate. You may also do this if you are not served a bread plate. However, never steal the bread plate of the person to your right, which may cause a domino effect around the table.

Utensil Usage

There are two acceptable ways of using silverware. One is the American way of shifting your fork from your left hand to your right hand, after you have made the cut. The other is the International style where you always keep your fork in your left hand, and your knife in the right. Either is acceptable in the United States of course, but the International style is more widely used, and acceptable wherever you are. Never use the American style while dining in Europe, as Europeans often do not understand the American way of doing things.

American Style: Hold the knife by the handle in the right hand with the index finger pointing toward the blade. Hold the fork in your left hand, with your forefinger on the back of the handle, with the tines facing downward. Pierce the meat with the fork, using the knife to cut off one bite at a time. Remove the fork from the meat, lay the knife on the right of the plate with the blade facing inward, and shift the fork to the right hand, placing your left hand in your lap. Keep the tines of the fork facing upward, and eat only one bite at a time.

International Style: Hold the knife and fork in the same manner as the American style, only don't put your knife down, and switch your fork to the right hand. Keep the tines of the fork facing downward at all times, and use the knife to help place the food on the fork.

Give it a try Pretend you are waving to a cute child with your thumb and fingers together, waving your fingers up and down. The very center of your palm, in the pocket you've created, is where the ends of your utensils go for the cutting position and for the International style of dining. Now, wrap your thumb and fingers around the utensil and place your index finger down the top. Handles in the hand – finger on the top!

When you have utensils in both hands for the cutting position or International style, the handles are always hiding in the pocket of the center of your palm. They are never peeking! The tines of the fork are always facing down.

When two utensils are used together, the handles are always hiding in the palm pocket, with the tines of the fork facing down. They are always both hiding, or they are placed in their resting or finished positions, but always together. Never put down one and hold the other while taking a sip of a drink, etc.

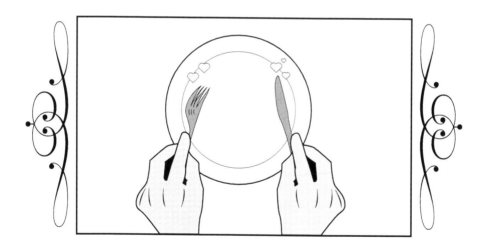

When only Ms. Fork is in use, her handle is out peeking, and not hiding. Her handle never hides in the palm pocket, but peeks out to see if she can spot Mr. Knife. Her tines are always up, never turned down like when she's being used with Mr. Knife. She also must be put down before you take a sip!

Remember – 2 Handles are always hiding and 1 is always peeking!

The resting position is the same for both the American and International styles of dining. The fork should cross over the knife, tines down, forming an X across the center of your plate. Never rest your cutlery on the sides of your plate like two oars off of a rowboat. Once a utensil has been used, it should never touch the table again. In the American style, it is also acceptable to rest your knife on the right side of the plate, with your fork at about a 4 o'clock position, tines up.

The finished position is also the same for both styles, with the fork and knife placed side-by-side, tines up or down, and blade facing inward, at the 5 o'clock position on your plate. Mr. Knife is always placed to the right of Ms. Fork, just as a gentleman would escort a lady. If a spoon is also used, such as for pasta, it goes to the left of Ms. Fork.

Ms. Fork and Mr. Knife always get together at 5 o'clock after a meal.

Never play with your silverware or anything else at the table and cause a disturbance, especially if you have finished and others are still eating. Please refrain from gesturing, or pointing with your cutlery and waving it in the air! Your utensils are to be used for eating and nothing more!

Always keep your elbows in while eating, especially when you are cutting something. We are humans, not chickens, so please do not flap your wings! Do not cut as though you are a cellist in a symphony!

General Dining Guidelines

1. Maintain good posture and sit up straight in your chair. Never rest your elbows on the table, or lean on the table. You may either place your hands in your lap, or balance your wrists on the edge of the table. The European style calls for your wrists to always be above the table.

2. Learn to bring the food to your mouth, not your mouth to the food. Avoid hovering over your plate and shoveling food into your mouth!

3. Champagne and white wine glasses are always held by the stem.

4. If you don't wish to have wine, do not turn your glass upside down or put a napkin on top. Simply wave your hand a bit and tell the server you don't care for wine. "You may remove my glass. I won't be having any wine this evening." If it is poured anyway, simply leave it there and ignore the glass.

5. Beverages are always picked up and sipped. Never leave the glass on the table and sip it out of a straw.

6. Always pour drinks into a glass from a can or bottle. A lady never drinks out of a can or bottle, unless that is the only thing available or the setting is very casual.

7. Do not suck your fingers, or ever put them into your mouth. Remeber "You can dine with a Princess or a Count, if you don't stick your fingers in your mouth!"

8. NEVER used your fingers to push food onto your fork!

9. Never lick your utensils! Even if it is the most delicious thing you have ever tasted, your spoon in not a lollipop!

10. Wait until everyone is finished with his or her meal before you leave the table, and properly excuse yourself.

11. Never push your plate away from you, or stack your plates!

12. Food is always passed to the right, starting with the host or

hostess. You should always be served on your left side, and cleared from the right. Only your beverages will be served to you on your right. When a platter of food is served to you, take a modest portion and place the serving spoon and fork back on the platter side-by-side, at the 5 o'clock position. Take the pieces nearest to you, and try not to poke around the platter looking for your favorite piece. If something is passed to you that you do not want, you may refuse it, but try not to leave yourself with an empty plate. Never let your host or hostess know that you don't like something that they have served. If you are a vegetarian, or are allergic to a certain type of food, be sure to notify your hosts beforehand, especially if you are the guest of honor. However, do not discuss your vegetarianism, diets or allergies at the dining table, as you may disgust or offend other guests.

13. Never reach for anything that is too far away from you. Politely ask for someone closer to it to pass it to you.

14. Pass the salt and pepper together, and set them down on the table rather than pass them mid-air. In many countries, it is believed that passing salt from one hand to another will pass bad luck to the other person. Therefore, first place the salt and pepper down on the table to break the cycle. Just like Mr. & Mrs. Knees, Mr. Salt & Ms. Pepper love each other very much and never wish to be separated!

15. Take small bites of food and try not to pack your mouth like a hamster. Chew quietly with your mouth closed, and if you are incapable of doing this – stay home until you learn how! Never speak with your mouth full. If you are asked a question, they will understand if you first finish chewing your food and then answer. Eat slowly, and thoroughly chew every bite. Food is meant to be enjoyed – so please don't rush!

16. Do not wipe your mouth on your sleeve or the back of your hand. Make sure to gently wipe your mouth and hands with your napkin whenever necessary. The napkin is your best friend at the table.

17. Spoon your soup away from you, skimming off the top layer, and then sip it from the side of your spoon. Please don't slurp! Remember the old saying: "As the ships go out to sea, I spoon my soup away from me." If a dish is served under your cup or bowl, place your spoon on it to the right side while in between bites and again when you are finished. This will safeguard you against catapulting a spoonful of soup or ice cream all over the guest across the table from you! If there is no plate beneath your bowl or cup, keep it inside of the vessel.

Spoons always rest on a plate if one is provided. Never leave a spoon inside of a dish.

18. Remove olive pits, fish bones, or anything else you need to remove from your mouth using your thumb and index finger. Without calling any attention to the situation, simply push the undesired object to the front of your mouth, and remove it using your thumb and forefinger. Do not spit it into your napkin, spit it out onto your plate, or drop it on the floor.

19. At formal settings most foods are eaten with a knife and fork, including chicken drumsticks and pizza. In casual dining however, you may use your hands, as long as you use Mr. Napkin and refrain from wiping your mouth and hands on your clothing!

20. Hamburgers and large sandwiches may be cut in half or quartered to be more manageable. Remember Mr. Napkin and be sure to use him often! Do not lick your fingers or wipe your mouth with the back of your hand.

21. Never rip open a packet of condiments with your teeth. Find the perforated edge and carefully pull it open with your fingers.

22. Never pick your teeth with a toothpick, your fingers, or anything else while at the table or where others can see you. Try to dislodge whatever it is with your tongue, by drinking some water, or excuse yourself to the restroom.

23. Do not put on make-up at the table. Certainly never brush your hair anywhere near a table, a kitchen, or anyplace where food is served.

24. The presence of a bug, hair, or any other revulsion should be dealt with in a quiet, civil manner. Do not make a scene and embarrass your host or fellow diners. Calmly and courteously point out the problem to your server, and ask to have it removed.

25. Always be courteous to those who serve you! Never be rude to anyone in public, and keep the feelings of others in mind.

26. When you have finished eating or asked if you would like more, never say "I'm full." Say, "I'm satisfied," or "No thank you, I've had enough."

27. When you are finished and others are still eating, do not allow the server to take your plate. It is rude to leave slower eaters with the only plates at the table. Keep your utensils in the resting position until you see that all fellow diners are also done. If a server is insistent, politely explain that you are still enjoying your meal.

Dessert

1. The utensils at the top of your plate are only for dessert, and should never be touched until dessert is served. If a server has not done it for you, <u>slide</u> the spoon and fork down to their respective positions (fork to left, spoon to right). Do not leave them at the top of your plate.

2. Anything served in a glass with a stem is eaten with a spoon. Hold the stem with one hand and spoon the dessert toward you, not away like you would soup. Rest the spoon inside of the glass only if a plate beneath is not provided. Always place it on the plate, to the right, for the resting and finished positions.

3. Cookies are never held and eaten whole. Break off bite size pieces from its position on the plate.

4. Cupcakes and muffins should be unwrapped and eaten with utensils, if they are provided. Otherwise, they should be eaten like a cookie, piece by piece.

5. Desserts with hard crusts or those that are difficult to eat, may be eaten with both the spoon and fork. Use the fork in your left hand to anchor it with the tines down, and eat it with the spoon in your right.

6. If you do not wish to have dessert, either quietly and politely decline it when it is served, or leave it alone. Your fellow diners need not hear about your diet and waistline.

Buffets

1. Wait for your host to signal that it is OK to begin the line. A good host will alert guests that the buffet is ready, lead guests to the buffet table, and hand out plates.

2. It is a good idea to find a seat before you get in line. You may hold your place by placing your drink down and your purse or jacket on the chair. Do not place anything on the table to hold your place. You may also drape the napkin on the chair arm or back, to signify that you are holding the place.

3. Make sure to put your drink down before you get in line. If that is impossible, hold it in your left hand, leaving your right free to serve yourself at the buffet. Purses, as always, remain on the left.

4. Most commonly you will find small plates in front of chafing dishes for the service utensils. Always place the service utensils back on this plate, even if the person in front of you left them inside of the dish.

5. Never pick at anything on your plate and put it into your mouth! Certainly do not pick anything out of a buffet dish and give it a taste. Nothing should be put in your mouth in a buffet line.

6. Once you have your plate, wait for others and sit down to-gether. Do not be the person who goes through the line first, eats, and then sits at the table with a full belly, dishes stacked, and napkin on the table while others are eating!

7. Politely ask a server to remove your plate if you are ready for seconds or the next course. If no servers are available, remove your plate to the nearest server's station or tray.

8. Try not to be a P.I.G. – Person Incredibly Gorging!

> ### *Remember*
> - Name tags are worn on the right just below the shoulder.
> - When mingling at events, hold beverages in your left hand, in order to keep your right free to shake hands.
> - Purses are always worn on the left for the same reason.

Toasting

Although it is not confirmed, legend has it that toasting came about due to worries about poisoning. A host would clink glasses with a guest, thereby spilling or exchanging some of the liquid into each other's glasses. They would then look each other in the eye and take a sip at the same time, exclaiming, "To your health." It is also said that clinking glasses came about in order to make enough noise to drive away evil spirits. Today, we toast in expressions of happiness, goodwill and in tribute. Here are some general rules and guidelines:

1. Do not clink glasses with the utensils to get guests' attention! Simply stand when you are ready to make the toast.

2. There is a definite art to giving a good toast, so please make sure you know what you are going to say before you stand. Toasts should not be read, nor should they be long winded.

3. To toast means to honor someone, not roast them.

4. Guests should always wait for the host or hostess to first make a toast. If you have a toast prepared, let your hostess know you would like to say something and ask them to let you know when would be the appropriate time.

5. Once a toast is made, everyone must raise their glass, clink if possible, take a sip and then put the glass down. If you do not take a sip before you put your glass down, it means you do not concur with what had been said.

Always take a sip before you put your glass down.

6. If a toast is made in your honor, do not stand, nor take a sip of your drink. You may say a toast in turn, "To my wonderful friends," and then take a sip.

7. Briefly look each person in the eye while you are clinking or raising glasses.

8. Many believe that it isn't proper to clink glasses, but rather you should just lift up your glass. Either way, you always make eye contact. Always defer to your host, and do the same. Clink, if clinking, lift, if lifting.

9. Champagne and white wine glasses are always held by the stem. You may also hold red wine glasses by the stem for the toast, in order to hear the resonance of the clinking of the crystal.

10. You may toast with most beverages, including your water. It does not have to be alcoholic. However, please refrain from using a tea or coffee cup for toasting.

11. If your glass is empty, do not ask the person to wait to give their toast until their glass is refilled. Just go through the motions and pretend to take a sip.

Fun Fact! - In the United States Navy, toasts are never to be made with water because superstition dictates that the person honored would be doomed to a watery grave. However, when toasts are made in honor of Prisoners of War or those Missing In Action, toasts are made with water because they did not have wine during captivity.

Tea & Coffee

There are volumes written about proper tea etiquette, but I will only touch on a few guidelines.

Fun fact - In ancient Rome, where food was mostly eaten with fingers, members of high society ate using 3 fingers, and the lower class ate using all five. The raised pinkie was a sign of elitism, and people would make a show of raising their pinkies, such as during tea, to make sure they were perceived as wealthy and cultured. Now, it is considered quite gauche to hold out your pinkie while sipping tea!

1. While seated at a dining table, tea and coffee will be poured on your right. If none is desired, then simply wave your hand and softly say, "No thank you" to the server. Do not turn your cup upside down or put a napkin over the top.

2. Teaspoons are used to gently stir, making sure to never clank the sides of the cup or make any noise whatsoever. It is then placed on the saucer behind the cup and never left inside. Please refrain from putting the spoon in your mouth before putting it down.

3. When you are served tea or coffee while seated at a dining table, the saucer always remains on the table. You never hold your cup and saucer at a dining table together in your hands. You would leave the saucer on the table and only pick up your cup.

$4.$ If using packets of sweeteners, do not rip them open with your teeth. Open them with your fingers, carefully pour the desired amount into your cup, then fold the paper and place it under your saucer. This hides the paper and keeps it from sticking to the bottom of your cup. If you are holding your cup and saucer, then place the folded packet on the back of your saucer.

$5.$ When seated at a settee, couch or at a coffee table, you may hold your saucer in your left hand and sip the tea with your right, or vice versa, if you are left handed.

$6.$ Purses are placed on your lap, by your feet, or against the chair back, never on top of the tea table.

$7.$ Tea time napkins are often smaller, and may be completely unfolded and placed across your lap.

$8.$ Always look into your cup while sipping your tea, not over it.

$9.$ Proper holding of a cup is with your index finger through the handle, with your thumb on top and middle finger below to steady it. Don't use two hands, unless you are using a cup with two handles, or none at all. Again, holding out your pinky is considered poor etiquette.

10. Tea sandwiches are eaten with 3 fingers. Never hold them with two hands. They are not eaten with a knife and fork.

11. Place curd, cream and jams on your plate. Use these condiments much like you would your bread and butter.

12. Milk and lemon are never used in tea together! Unlike Mr. & Mrs. Knees, milk and lemon are not in love, and never wish to be together, or they curdle and fight!

13. It is widely controversial, but the milk is traditionally poured into the cup **before** the tea.

14. Please do keep Mr. & Mrs. Knees in mind, especially when seated on a low chair or couch. They do hate to be apart!

Thank you for reading *Urbanity Fair - An Abbreviated Guide to Modern Manners*. I hope you found it to be enlightening, if not just a brush up on what you already know.

When I reflect upon etiquette and its true meaning, I am more inclined to think of it as a guideline by which to live, in order to lead happier, more fulfilling lives. Showing common courtesies to others makes us a little kinder, gentler and perhaps a bit more understanding of one another.

More than anything, I hope you come away with a heightened sense of need for interpersonal communication, without a screen. Innately, we are all social creatures and we need human interaction. Please make an effort to put down your phone and actually engage in conversation. Nurture your relationships and do not take them for granted. After all, the cornerstones of kindness, respect, appreciation and love are the only things that can bring us true happiness.

Never underestimate a smile, a door held open, or a simple hand-written note. They could make someone's day or even change a life. Who knows, that life just might be yours.

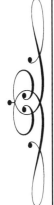

For more information and
instructional videos please visit

www.**urbanityfair**.net

About The Author

Julie Ann Ulcickas has been teaching the art of etiquette since 1992. From a young age, she has been trained in the many facets of etiquette through various schools and social organizations. She was a member of The National Charity League for six years, a National Charity League Debutante, a La Canada Thursday Club Les Fleurettes Debutante and a 1988 Tournament of Roses Princess. She ran Happy Girlz Finishing School, teaching etiquette, poise, carriage, health, nutrition, and beauty to girls. She wrote a monthly column entitled "Manners, Taste, & Social Grace", for the La Canada Outlook Newspaper, was the etiquette expert for "Coast Kids Magazine", and has been featured on radio and television. She teaches at a multitude of Clubs in the LA and Orange County areas, as well as Scout troops, Debutantes, National Charity League, the National League of Young Men, her Kappa Kappa Gamma sorority at USC, and private engagements. She is also the etiquette and modeling trainer for the Tournament of Roses Royal Court®. Julie Ann resides in Orange County with her husband Jim, owner of Bluewater Grill restaurants and their two children, Frank and Ella.

37852468R00038

Made in the USA
Middletown, DE
03 March 2019